Herbert Lewis Kruse Blunck

Form and Technology

Preface by
Tom Beeby, FAIA
Introduction by
Filippo Beltrami Gadola

Chief Editor of Collection
Maurizio Vitta

Publishing Coordinator
Franca Rottola

Editorial Staff
Cristina Rota

Graphic Design
Studio Manolibera snc, Milano

Editing
Martyn J. Anderson

Colour-Separation
Litofilms Italia, Bergamo

Printing
Bolis Poligrafiche Spa, Bergamo

First published November 2001

Copyright 2001
by l'Arca Edizioni

ISBN 88-7838-101-2

Contents

Preface

by Tom Beeby, FAIA

Iowa is the gridded center of the United States in most Americans' minds. What could be more American than Iowa? In my mind "American Gothic" by Grant Wood rises as a compelling image of the power of Iowa to create the heroic form from the ordinary. The Des Moines Art Center by Eliel Saarinen possesses true monumentality in its simple use of materials and elimination of the unnecessary while sustaining an aura of warmth and community. The works of Grant Wood fit into this building comfortably, for they project the same sensibility. Indeed if one treasures Iowa there are amazing wonders hidden in fertile fields and tidy towns.

In Ames, at Iowa State University are found the astounding murals by Grant Wood that portray the settlers engaged in everyday tasks while possessing the grace and repose of a Piero della Francesca saint. Similarly at Cedar Rapids the stained glass window created by the same artist shows the sheltering female figure of the same Piero luminously enfolding the hauntingly tragic figures of the war dead from Iowa's past. Radiant faces of farm boys gaze bravely into your eyes portraying the willingness to die to protect one's own. Grant Wood has taken forms received from elsewhere and transformed them into an evocation of Midwestern memories.

Diagonally across the street and river the intense little bank structure by Louis Sullivan is protected by guardian lions almost sinister in their determination to safeguard the savings of the town. Further west in Grinnell another bank by Sullivan glistens like a shimmering jewel box opened to display its riches. Simultaneously, crouching lions again guard the doors as a warning to those who would steal from the worthy. How appropriate that when the worldly large cities to the east tired of Sullivan, the long suppressed romantic nature of German Protestant culture coupled with its worthy descendent found in Yankee Transcendentalism would engage him here and ask him to create his most poetic works for them.

To the north in Mason City Frank Lloyd Wright created his masterly bank complex, the building that inspired Walter Gropius to change the course of European architecture forever. At Rock Glen in this same small city a parade of late Prairie Style houses by Walter Burley Griffin suggest where the architecture of Midwest might have gone if he had not been drawn to Australia. Invention in detail and material that could have moved beyond while still sustaining the power of craft.

Even Mies van der Rohe, (who as myth suggests) loved Iowa for its flatness, built his beautiful little urban bank in Des Moines. This is the other side of the German/Yankee character. The mind-set that creates a world receiving its power from reduction rather than elaboration. Here necessity is transformed through denial of all that is not absolutely essential into a hauntingly simple poem based on need. The grid that shapes the land and community is distilled here into a structural architecture that informs the building at all levels of detail.

I would suggest that the work of Herbert Lewis Kruse Blunck has much to do with the artistic traditions described above. Always starting with the requirement of the task at hand, the buildings develop pragmatically as a direct response to need. This is where all Midwestern architecture starts, for the roots of our culture demand this. However, in the best work of Central United States a reflex condition evolves that demands poetic intervention to raise the work above being merely workmanlike, to move the onlooker to a higher plane of comprehension. It would seem that this creative reaction has more to do with matters of the spirit than art for it is executed in all seriousness with no sense of play.

I believe the work of Herbert Lewis Kruse Blunck is conceived and built in this atmosphere and by doing so not only draws on this honoured tradition but also has the opportunity to extend its legacy well into the future. This is a path that is difficult to follow for it demands great discipline but its rewards are felt by the entire region in a most profound way.

Introduction

by Filippo Beltrami Gadola

Herbert Lewis Kruse Blunck's architecture basically focuses on the American urban environment, successfully coming up against and, at the same time, to terms with issues mainly linked to the city and urban redevelopment. All this happens in a place like the U.S., where history and space have always set new and innovative design paradigms.

The best way of examining the context in which this firm from Des Moines, Iowa works is to imagine a map of the United States. Four different time zones run vertically across the boundless American landscape from coast to coast, following meandering paths and overlapping the almost rigidly geometric borders of its endless counties: this is how the current signs of Jefferson's dream of rural America now appear to anyone peering down on this immense country from above, carefully drawn with a rule and compass in a benevolent natural environment governed by science and reason, where natural boundaries, mountains, and rivers provide little opposition to a desire to develop and control.

All those who have keenly followed how this adventure has gradually evolved with real interest and sincere amazement cannot help remembering those pictures collected by Reps depicting the key episodes in the constitution of a potential urban nation, as the dawning of a civilization revealed itself in its entirety in an attempt to provide coherent responses to more general issues related to the founding of a city and its future development, its relations to a still largely wild and mysterious land, and the infinite possibilities opened up by experimentation. Few in the history of mankind have found themselves with such a burden of responsibility: a blank sheet of almost totally virgin territory offering the chance to try out different ways of sustaining seemingly unstoppable, high speed economic growth. The urban heart of the American continent, the heir to what is now a centuries-old history, has taken giant steps over the last few decades, so that it can now offer or even export its own peculiar means of growth and development.

In this context, Herbert Lewis Kruse Blunck's architecture represents the most recent work of an architectural firm deeply entrenched in constructing the image and determining the prospects of a city in the Midwest, which has significantly been described as one of the region's most pleasant to live in. The city can boast a brief but complicated history, whose origins may be traced back to the great Chicago Exhibition in 1892. The exhibition to commemorate the four-hundredth anniversary of the discovery of America by Europeans actually marked, as many people have noted, the start not so much and not only of America's own autonomous school of architecture and town-planning, as the actual realization of this autonomy: the grid, chequer board, symbol and starting point, and solutions (in all their different variations) capable of quickly adapting to models of growth imposed by development and deriving in part from Greek and Roman styles that the American Revolution was so fond of, are among its most obvious results. The so-called urban block, capable of both adapting to all the different morphological features of the land and, at the same time, proposing ideal spatial-geometric solutions for urban growth in every imaginable direction, is the system's single-cell organism capable of hosting the widest possible assortment of building types, regardless of the size of the buildings it holds. A culture actually rather lacking in qualities able to translate the need for communal urban spaces along the lines of a Mediterranean urban centre expresses its own civic values through stylistic models which have only recently appeared on the scene.

Herbert Lewis Kruse Blunck's architecture seems to work around providing solutions suitably geared to this state of affairs. The need to move beyond the rigid imposition of the urban grid, without just rejecting it outright a priori, and to create spaces for new forms of social life and provide community spaces for everyday goings-on in civil life are the real challenges currently facing architectural design. Despite the hyper-technological temptations of the "global village", cities everywhere, not just in America, are claiming their right to catalyse modern-day people's social activities, at the same time delving down within themselves to find non-virtual, physical places capable of coping with this almost unexpected turn-around.

This is the rugged but fertile terrain on which the Herbert Lewis Kruse Blunck firm moves with such skill and precision. Its' works, emblematically outlined in this publication, derive from this vision of the cityscape as a place of community relations, communication, and interaction. Major urban spaces like Kautz Plaza at the University of Iowa, the Site Development of the American College Testing Program in Iowa City or the Richard O. Jacobson Athletic Building for the Football Program Space, again at the University of Iowa, are all organised more around town-planning criteria than architectural lines; and even though the Herbert Lewis Kruse Blunck team devises its projects around the internal functions of its works, the buildings still manage to make their presence felt on the surrounding environment, even managing to shape its physical appearance.

The roots of this approach to design focusing around urban aesthetics can easily be traced back to the inspiring influence of the City Beautiful Movement. Once again Chicago, the capital of the Midwest makes itself felt, the city for which Daniel Burnham envisaged a monumental future: the city as a work of art full of symbolic buildings reflecting the ambitions of a growing nation. This probably marks the start of a long process of urban-scale design in the United States: the idea of the city as a mechanism capable of re-adapting to an aesthetic model shared, as far as possible, by its inhabitants; a sense of belonging based on the grounding idea that the city may and must be constructed out of elements capable of injecting the entire system with its own clear-cut identity.

The furthermost inland States of the USA are still in some respects hard to grasp. Most notably, the Midwest, an in-between land, a place for potentially knitting together both coasts armed with big cities that seem to stretch out endlessly, seems to have been bent on discretely hiding away its own nature and distinctive features. Herbert Lewis Kruse Blunck's architecture is, to some extent, a way of revealing these secrets. It contains all the familiar themes of the Modern Movement and its subsequent developments in the latter half of the 20th century: works of architecture designed with rigorous geometric precision, the focusing on orthogonal lines and volumes, and the perfectly functional organization of interior space. Moreover, each work of architecture, starting with the Center Street Park & Ride Facility in Des Moines or, in other respects, Praxair Distribution in Ankeny, exudes an all-American sense of stylistic pragmatism, where architecture is no longer designed around the spiritualistic principle of the European *Gestaltung*, but rather a genuine concern for practical requirements, finding reasonable solutions to problems, and the ability to meet real needs.

Each project designed by Herbert Lewis Kruse Blunck has its own story to tell, an independent stylistic process capable of adjusting to the widest imaginable range of specific technical-social needs. Their architecture seems to be suggesting and proposing means of catering for new life styles, little more than experimental social models geared to architecture conceived as a way of positively influencing human behaviour and psycho-physical well-being. This means that careful attention is paid to interaction between light and shadow, and the distribution/designation of forms and colours: design encourages, invites, and persuades, without ever imposing or enforcing itself. Hardly surprisingly, the monumental side of the buildings lies in their human scale and in how architecture relates to its potential users.

Industrial-type building systems are another leit-motif, frequently used without false modesty to emphasise the solidity and clarity of a finished work of architecture. Building aesthetics treated as an intricate piece of productive, functioning and functional machinery pervade the firm's architectural work: the city is furbished with everything it needs to function smoothly, presenting its inhabitants with a ponderous image of gracefulness, the concrete results of technological research applied to building materials.

Architecture seems, ultimately, to be designed to use the means at its disposal to send out a message of a new sense of professional ethics, a carefully balanced combination of man and machine, work and leisure. There is a pervasive sense of having to find new paths through working environments: flights of stairs leading up to the light, enclosed spaces whose size can be altered according to various needs, and places dedicated to communal company life.

Nevertheless, Herbert Lewis Kruse Blunck's architecture is not confined to the working environment: major sports facilities on the University of Iowa campus, for instance, are an important part of the firm's architectural repertoire. They physically embody real traces of academic life, whose own almost natural connections with cutting-edge technology and research fit in neatly with the ambitions of an American state. In the United States, university sport plays a crucial part in forming a sense of national pride, and here, as elsewhere, the facilities also serve symbolic purposes. This explains the care and attention with which new or redeveloped spaces are created, always relying on a clever and carefully-gauged choice of forms and colours: a vigorous almost heroic approach to design, well aware of the intrinsic meaning of a person's intellectual development.

It is also worth remembering other works more directly related to creative activities, such as the "Objects of Art" shop, the offices of Engineering Animation Inc., or the studio and other facilities of Sticks Inc. Herbert Lewis Kruse Blunck's architecture is carefully and discretely geared to every aspect of culture, embodying artistic values in a subtle structural idiom mirroring its image and projecting its meanings.

After all, this is the most significant lesson American architecture has to teach us. Newly built architectural complexes do not derive from factors related to form and function. Design and composition actually seem to work around quite different paradigms, such as recognizability and the need to provide an effective work of architecture at the same time capable of acting as a potential local landmark. The basic idea is to create explicit architecture, which does not require any sort of initiation process in order to be understood: pragmatism here means providing the right answers to certain questions. Design aesthetics like these are entrenched in the truth of forms and building materials, the right layout of spaces, and carefully gauged relations between individual buildings and the surrounding city.

Works

Iowa City, Iowa
1989

North Campus Parking and Chilled Water Facility
University of Iowa

Date Completed:
1989

Owner:
State Board of Regents, State of
Iowa, University of Iowa

Ground Area:
1.27 acres

Constructed Area:
200,765 Gross Square Feet (400 cars)

Architectural Design:
Herbert Lewis Kruse Blunck
Architecture

General Contractor:
The Weitz Company

Structural:
Charles Saul Engineering

Mechanical / Electrical:
Stanley Consultant

Cost Estimator:
The Construction Consulting
Group, L.T.D .

Parking:
Walker Parking Consultants

Collaboration:
NA

Photographer:
Farshid Assassi

The project for this multi-purpose facility is based on the premise that even urban design can achieve a reasonable level of stylistic elegance. The building in question, a multi-storey car park, holds a vast array of different functions: a central water chiller plant, an electricity sub-station, a reservoir serving Iowa City, and a recreation deck, all situated in close vicinity to a university accommodation block.

Its location cleverly exploits the geo-physical features of the site, so as to minimize the structure's overall visual impact on the surrounding architectural structures and diminish the effects deriving from its undeniable stylistic difference.

The tricky design programme has been translated into careful attention to construction details, which are treated with simple, sober elegance, and great care over pedestrian circulation problems. The unusual nature of its aesthetic force is full of meaning: the cars are camouflaged behind the use of a light-weight metal grille injecting the complex with a technologically efficient image. Great attention if focused on the stairwell/lift shaft with a metallic grey-coloured structure running vertically through it, and featuring intricately designed banisters.

Opening page, the stairwell/lift shaft visually anchors the facility to the site and serves as a significant campus pedestrian path for student travel.
Right, site plan indicating the diversity of components incorporated into facility.
Below, by carefully inserting the structure into the sloped site, the facility blends with the urban landscape and serves as a recreation area for the adjacent residence halls.

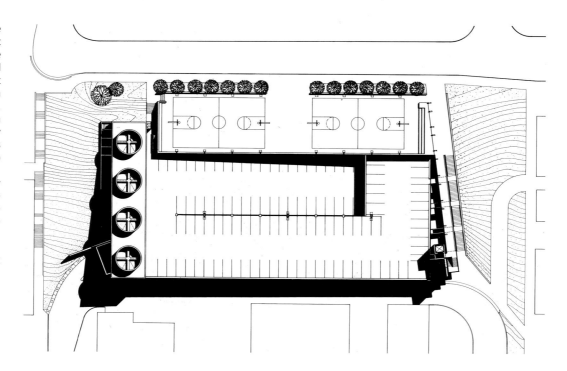

The accessible bridge, stairwells, and lift shaft form a recognizable and sculpture pedestrian pathway against the campus horizon.

A glass enclosed lift shaft provides a sense of security to users, while taking part in the views to the campus beyond.

Iowa City, Iowa
1995

Kautz Plaza
University of Iowa

Date Completed:
1995

Owner:
State Board of Regents, State of
Iowa, University of Iowa

Ground Area:
41 acres

Constructed Area:
NA

Architectural Design:
Herbert Lewis Kruse Blunck
Architecture

General Contractor:
Suburban Contractors

Structural:
Shive Hattery, Inc.

Mechanical / Electrical:
Shive Hattery, Inc.

Landscape:
Crose Gardner

Cost Estimator:
CMPI, Inc.

Paving:
Suburban Contractors

Collaboration:
NA

Photographer:
Farshid Assassi

The completion of a pedestrian path through the facilities on the University of Iowa campus accounts for the creation of this interesting "quasi-urban" space designed to construct something that would fill the left-over space.

Large university complexes, growing not only qualitatively but, also and most significantly, in terms of size, are undergoing deep internal changes, making them ideal candidates for representing an urban image and acting as authentic "cities within the city", following a similar path and facing the same basic contradictions and development procedures.

In this case, there are close links between "problems" and their "solution", as part of a working method in which architecture seems to naturally take on the rule of providing an effective means of restating the problem.

This is the familiar issue of creating a community place equipped with the services and structures required to allow its users (in this case students) to go about their daily lives, but also serving plenty of other purposes: stairs, walls, platforms, and urban furnishing, all located in an area whose geometric layout is carefully gauged, form the pieces of a complicated puzzle working along unitary lines.

Opening page, a stainless steel plate fastened to the canopy structure with simple socket-head fasteners serves as the guardrail for the central stair. Right, vicinity plan of the surrounding campus with the five-building "pentacrest" to the south and the student union and riverfront to the west. The plaza resolves the crossing of two established pedestrian pathways. Below, the perforated canopy casts an ever-changing shadow pattern on the limestone wall below.

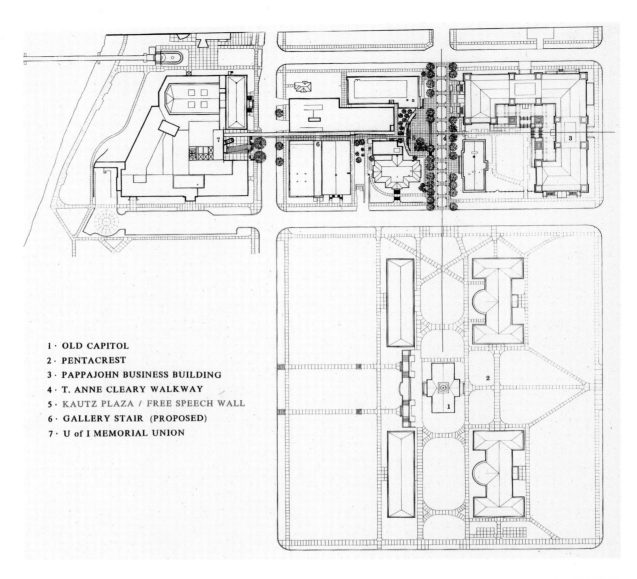

1 · OLD CAPITOL
2 · PENTACREST
3 · PAPPAJOHN BUSINESS BUILDING
4 · T. ANNE CLEARY WALKWAY
5 · KAUTZ PLAZA / FREE SPEECH WALL
6 · GALLERY STAIR (PROPOSED)
7 · U of I MEMORIAL UNION

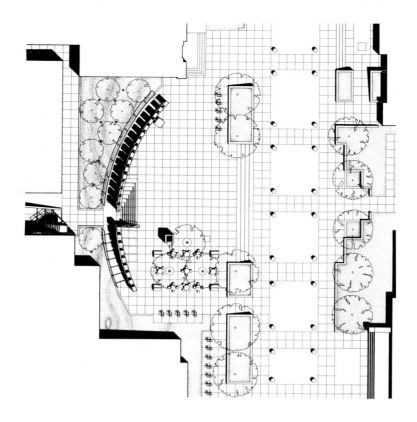

Left, site plan of Kautz Plaza and the adjacent Clary Walkway.
Below left, a curved ramp provides access to the plaza for the physically disabled. More utilitarian facades of buildings beyond are effectively screened by the new construction.
Below right, the end of the limestone wall adjacent to the central stair. The stainless steel speaker's platform is visible in the distance.

**Ankeny, Iowa
1993**

Date Completed:
1993

Owner:
Perishable Distributors of Iowa

Ground Area:
4.1 acres

Constructed Area:
14,000 Gross Square Feet + 8,000
Gross Square Feet existing
remodel

Architectural Design:
Herbert Lewis Kruse Blunck
Architecture

General Contractor:
Taylor Ball

Structural:
Charles Saul Engineering

Mechanical:
Taylor Industries

Electrical:
Tesdell Electric

Collaboration:
NA

Photographer:
Farshid Assassi

Perishable Distributors of Iowa, Office Addition and Interiors

The project designed for Perishable Distributors of Iowa took the form of an extension to the offices and warehouses of a company involved in the distribution and wholesale of perishable foods. The design worked around the now familiar issue of carefully devising a logistical/organisational system geared around flexible service spaces.

The architectural design works around the need to provide a credible project falling within the set budget and building schedule and resulted in the adoption of construction features already found in the existing building. The steel structural frame is deliberately exposed, and the building materials, including glass blockwork and masonry, are also clearly on show almost everywhere.

The new addition features a public entrance through a circular mass of glass blockwork, while the interiors are divided into three areas: the management zone in the north section facing outwards through a set of regular apertures, a central section holding the work stations, and a southern section abutting the existing warehouse holding the cafeteria, meeting room, and gym.

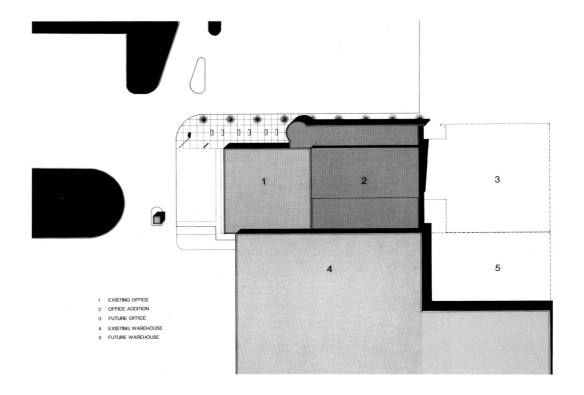

1 EXISTING OFFICE
2 OFFICE ADDITION
3 FUTURE OFFICE
4 EXISTING WAREHOUSE
5 FUTURE WAREHOUSE

Opening page, a glass block cylinder marks the new entry to the office complex. The ice block image of the glass units make a light-hearted reference to the company's refrigeration warehouse.
Above, site plan.
Below left, simple industrial materials were used to exploit the project's inherent warehouse aesthetic.
Below right, light admitted through the glass block circulation spine and wedge of clerestory windows keeps the interior environment bright, despite the large floorplate of the building.

Left, the desk in the reception area is a playful homage to the cardboard boxes used in the shipping function of the warehouse.
Below left, the openness of the office area is an expression of PDI's commitment to an accessible managerial style.
Below right, exploded axonometric.

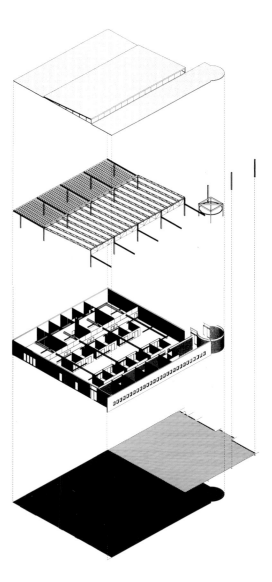

Homeland Savings Bank

Date Completed:
1995

Owner:
Homeland Savings Bank

Ground Area:
1.51 acres

Constructed Area:
4,500 0

Architectural Design:
Herbert Lewis Kruse Blunck
Architecture

General Contractor:
Taylor Ball

Structural:
Charles Saul Engineering

Mechanical / Electrical:
Stroh Corporation

Collaboration:
NA

Photographer:
Farshid Assassi

The design of this branch Bank for Homeland Savings is connected to the idea of developing and expanding the suburban community of Greater Des Moines. The building stands in close vicinity to a busy highway and successfully meets the client's needs: on one hand, providing the branch with a solid, efficient image and, on the other, making it easily recognisable to passing motorists.

The building is constructed around a 20-foot-high, 140-foot-long wall projecting into the bank and carefully organising the public entrance in the form of both a "walk in" design and "drive up" facility. This connecting wall, constructed out of cement board panels mechanically fastened to a weather-tight substrate, gives the complex a visually striking image, making it look as if it is built out of large units of stone masonry.

Most significantly, it was decided to a construct large windows to let plenty of natural light into the building; the same attention was more generally paid to the materials (brick, cement, and steel), which are carefully combined with what can only be described as extraordinary balance.

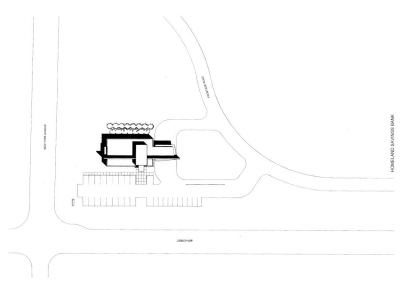

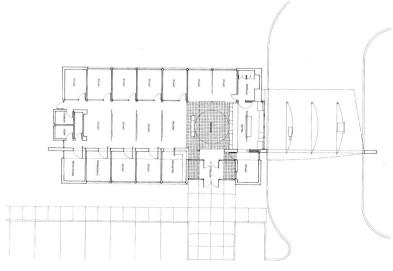

Above, vicinity/site plan.
Opening page, the 140-
foot long wall,
recognizable from
passing automobiles and
evident on the interior of
the structure, provides
the unifying visual
element for the bank.
Below, the drive-up
facility is announced and
visually supported by the
140-foot wall, which
organizes the plan.

Above, floor plan at
street level.
Below, clerestory light
brightens the interior
and allows the wall to
visually pass through the
structure.

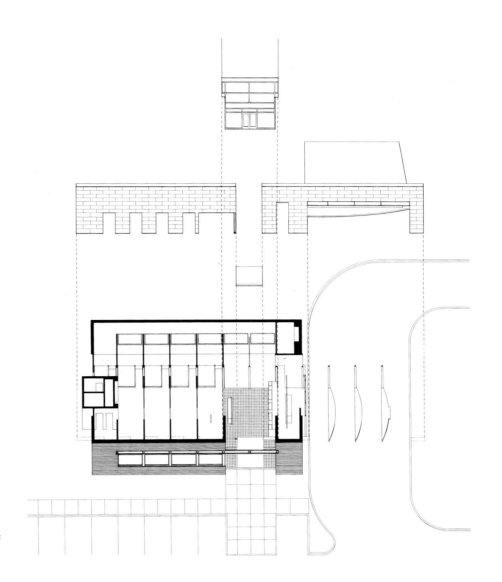

Right, exploded axonometric indicating the organizational concept of the wall. The interior organization and detail reflects the character of the exterior.

A tall volume and clerestory light welcome visitors to the walk-in facility.

**Iowa City, Iowa
1995**

Richard O. Jacobson Athletic Building, Addition and Interiors
University of Iowa

Date Completed:
1995

Owner:
State Board of Regents, State of Iowa, University of Iowa

Ground Area:
2.7 acres

Constructed Area:
36,900 Gross Square Feet New Construction, 7,000 Gross Square Feet Remodeled Construction

Architectural Design:
Herbert Lewis Kruse Blunck Architecture

General Contractor:
Mid-America Construction

Structural:
Shuck Britson, Inc.

Mechanical / Electrical:
Alvine & Associates

Programmer:
Sink Combs Dethlafs, P.C.

Mechanical Contractor:
Tom Barker & Son

Electrical Contractor:
Meisner Electric Company

Collaboration:
NA

Photographer:
Farshid Assassi

The clarity of the entry facade is a main feature of the new building extension to the University of Iowa football program, an approximately 37,000-square-foot facility designed to update the strength training and sports medicine facilities, locker rooms, and support facilities.

The complex holds plenty of free spaces organised for hosting sports activities, where the industrial-style elements of the bearing structure really stand out: huge areas projecting upwards and filled with athletic equipment are set out in a neat pattern. The outside elevations are cleverly designed with large walls of horizontal corrugated metal panels gently sloping to evoke dynamic geometric forms crowned near the top by wide glass spaces.

The entrance can be recognised by a huge battered grey wall supporting a metal canopy and continuing into the building lobby. The interplay of colours characterising the closed spaces is particularly important: the white walls and ceilings, the large yellow entrance doors to the training areas, and the various shades of grey on the floors and inside curtain walls.

Opening page, entry canopy and vestibule with rooftop banners. Opposite page above, clerestory windows and indirect lighting provide even illumination in the strength training room.

Opposite page below, openings puncture the battered wall at the entry.
Below, entry plaza in the evening.
Bottom, elevation view with entry plaza in the foreground.

Oversized doors mark the entry into the strength training area.

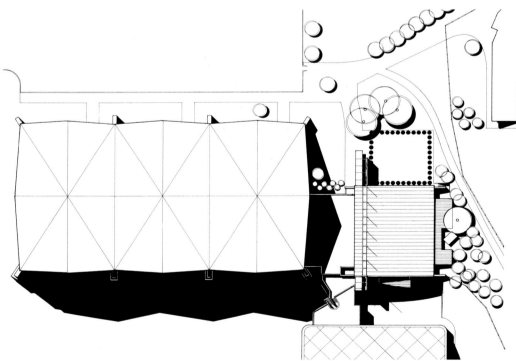

Site plan with existing athletic building, office wing, and the new addition.

Opposite page, the battered wall at the entrance continues through the reception hall.

**Ames, Iowa
1996**

Date Completed:
1996 (phase 1) 2000 (phases 2, 3
and 3A)

Owner:
Engineering Animation, Inc.

Ground Area:
10.7 acres

Constructed Area:
95,700 Gross Square Feet (Total all
phases)

Architectural Design:
Herbert Lewis Kruse Blunck
Architecture

General Contractor:
CPMI Construction

Structural:
Bossenburger Associates

Mechanical:
ACI Mechanical Corporation

Electrical:
Meisner Electric

Developer:
CPMI-CRE, Inc.

Construction Manager:
CPMI, Inc.

Collaboration:
Roseland Architects

Photographers:
Farshid Assassi
Hedrich Blessing

Engineering Animation, Inc.

This headquarters of a national computer animation firm located inside the incubator campus of a large university in the Midwest is situated between a highway and a natural pond. The architectural complex is perceived as a clever juxtaposition of forms and colours, openings and curtain walls. The elevations' elegant classicism, featuring a vertical pattern of large windows, makes them look rather linear.

A large dark translucent mass, a polished structure masterfully used to reinforce the connection between the complex's exterior appearance and technological function and also holding, in striking contrast, the entrance to the main building, welcomes visitors and gives the complex a deliberately simple image. The lobby in the very heart of the building acts as the organisational hub for the interiors, carefully separating spaces and functions.

The interior layout is constructed around a triple partition forcefully mirroring the building's form in its outside elevations: large clear-coloured structural veils emerge from the main block, thrusting up to inject a sense of dynamism into the facades. The architectural core opens up toward the pond, where there are rest areas. The presentation room's panoramic glass wall looks onto the pond.

The interior, on the other hand, is designed to carefully separate public and non-public activities through cleverly thought-out spatial divisions. The enclosed premises work around the idea of large structures: the stairs leading up to the presentation room looks like a huge gap of monumental proportions, further underlined by the correct choice of colours. The metal and stone in different shades of grey create a sense of sober elegance and peaceful productivity.

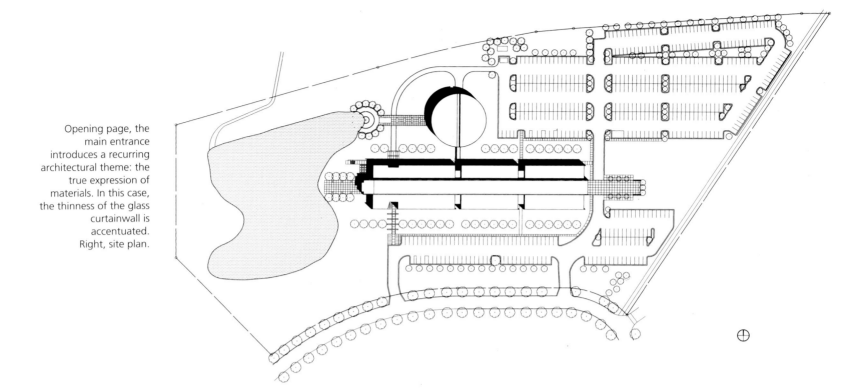

Opening page, the main entrance introduces a recurring architectural theme: the true expression of materials. In this case, the thinness of the glass curtainwall is accentuated. Right, site plan.

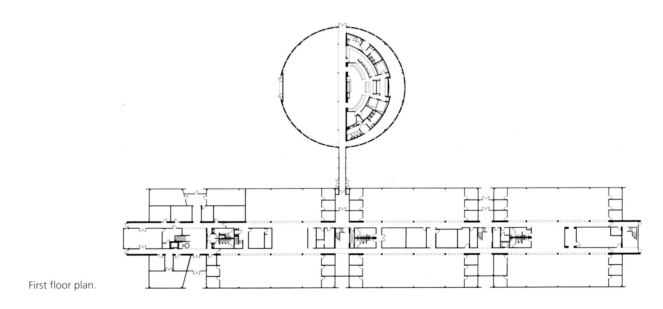

First floor plan.

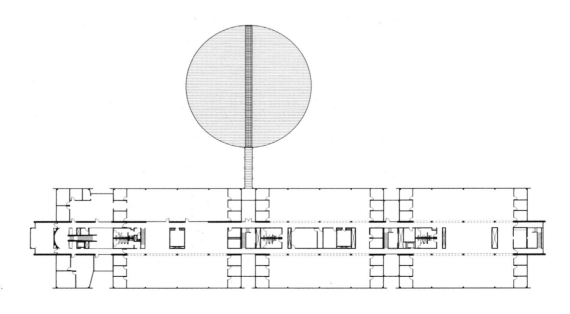

Second floor plan.

Organization and function are expressed through materials - black glass shields computer monitors from direct sun, corrugated metal defines circulation.

The knife-edge expression of the black glass plane is complemented by a row of locust trees sited in the middle of the yard to reflect in the glass facade and reinforce a linearity .

Left, the building's end elevation contains public spaces which overlook a plaza and pond.
Below from left, stair to second level conference room and executive suite; in the upper lobby, the linearity of varying materials is clearly expressed; maple walls create towering vertical planes in the main lobby; circulation is defined by the corrugated metal walls. A floating ceiling becomes the building's main cable raceway.

Ankeny, Iowa
1996

Praxair Distribution

Date Completed:
1996

Owner:
Praxair Distribution

Ground Area:
NA - existing space remodel

Constructed Area:
22,600 Gross Square Feet (office, conference, training)
38,600 Gross Square Feet (warehouse and distribution)

Architectural Design:
Herbert Lewis Kruse Blunck Architecture

General Contractor:
Neumann Brothers

Structural:
Charles Saul Engineering

Mechanical / Electrical:
Stroth Corporation

Collaboration:
NA

Photographer:
Farshid Assassi

The project is based around the conversion of an industrial building. A 58,000-square-foot warehouse inside a manufacturing district has been transformed into a centre for welding supplies.

One third of the facility houses the office, conference and training operations, while the balance is warehouse space. The industrial nature of the operation is expressed by deliberately leaving the original structure exposed. The necessary stylistic unity running through the entire building takes concrete form in a uniform choice of building/construction materials.

The complex's industrial nature is underlined and embellished; the entire building looks like an efficient manufacturing machine shot through with the chromatic effects of metal and the opaque severity of the curtain elements.

Translucent walls and exposed roofs set the stylistic rhythm of the interiors incorporating openly flaunted technological systems as an integral part of the entire system.

Opening page, the industrial aesthetic and grand scale of the existing warehouse are highlighted in the new office area for this distributor of industrial gas products.
Right, plan diagram showing the new office conversion serving the existing warehouse space.
Below, the new entrance shares daylight and displays product.

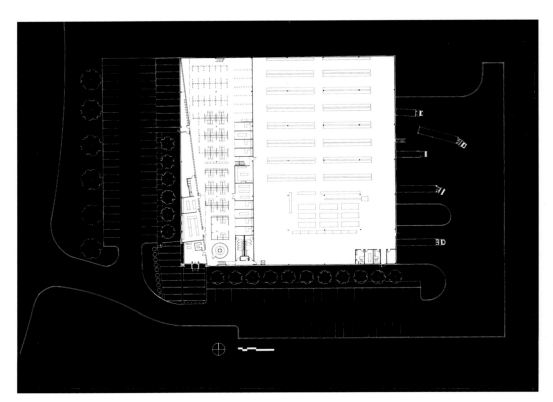

A translucent light wall zones the space and introduces daylight into the warehouse.

A cylindrical conference room helps mark the entry into the office area.

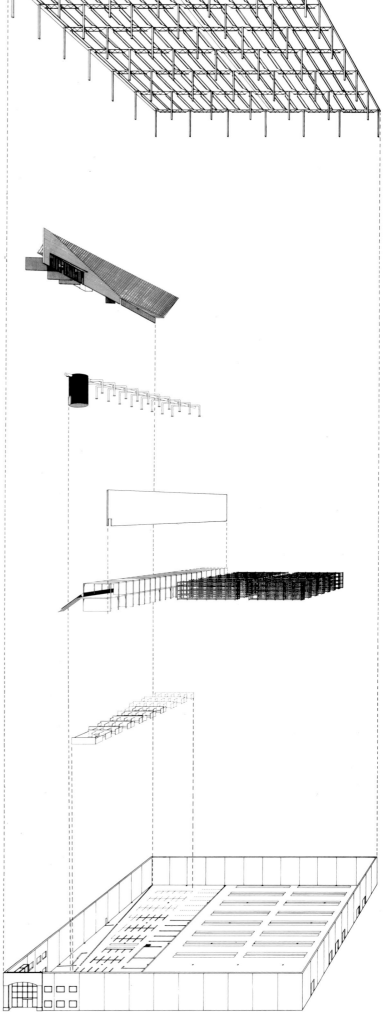

Above, air distribution and light become features inside the conference cylinder. Right, exploded axonometric identifying the critical systems of the facility. Opposite page, the cylindrical conference room and duct work recall the storage tank and distribution system used in the company's gas canister filling operation.

Right, the industrial shelving used in the warehouse also forms and structures the office area and mezzanine. Opposite page, the folded planes of the light wall create a rigid structure while providing a dynamic source of daylight along the entire length of the facility.

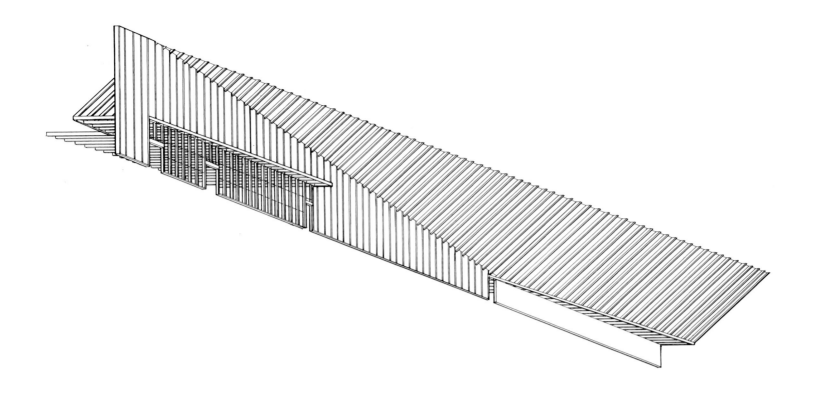

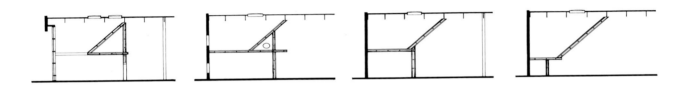

From top, diagram of the folded light wall plane; sections of the structural triangulation supporting the light wall. Right and opposite page, the grand scale of the light wall creates a dominant presence in the interior.

Equitable of Iowa Companies

Date Completed:
1998

Owner:
Equitable of Iowa Companies

Ground Area:
1.9 acres

Constructed Area:
240,000 Gross Square Feet
(building and shell only)

Architectural Design:
Herbert Lewis Kruse Blunck
Architecture

General Contractor:
Graham Construction

Structural:
Dennis & Magnani Structural
Consultants

Civil:
Bishop Engineering

Mechanical:
Baker Mechanical

Electrical:
Baker Electric

Collaboration:
NA

Photographer:
Farshid Assassi

The Equitable of Iowa building is in the downtown business district of the city of Des Moines. The office covers a commercial surface area of 240,000 square feet over six floors above grade and also has an underground car park with room for about one hundred cars, all connected to the downtown core by an overhead pedestrian walkway.

The elevations are constructed out of carefully chosen limestone and a masonry and steel composition, while the interiors are designed around the client's need for efficient, flexible office spaces. The northern section of the building lot, currently occupied by an unused car park, can cater for further extensions to the finished construction.

This compact-looking building is bordered by roads on three sides: the ground floor is decorated with a pattern of wide glass openings and the four upper levels feature an elegant set of windows leading up to the stylistically varied top floor, where polished metal elements are designed in the same pattern found on the ground floor. The complex terminates near the top in a huge overhanging screen capable of injecting motion into the vertical thrust of the elevations.

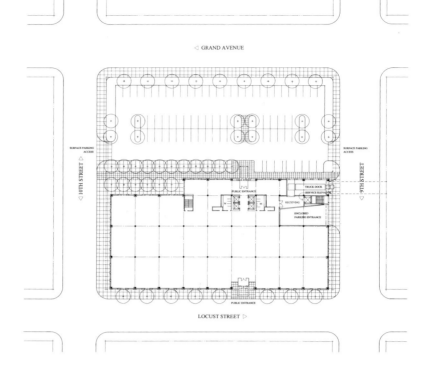

Opening page, the public entrance is located on the quarter point of the block-long facade, thereby breaking down the visual mass of the structure.
Above, site plan.
Below, the building was developed to accommodate future expansion. The public skywalk concourse and service functions are housed in the 20 foot-wide enclosure constructed over the vacated alley.

Left, the service mass is simply constructed of glass and black masonry. Below, limestone, brick masonry, glass, and a steel fabricated cornice make up the material composition of the building shell.

Ames, Iowa
1996

Athletic Office and Training Facility
Iowa State University

Date Completed:
1996

Owner:
State Board of Regents, State of Iowa, Iowa State University

Ground Area:
NA

Constructed Area:
43,000 Gross Square Feet (new), 38,000 Gross Square Feet (remodeled)

Architectural Design:
Herbert Lewis Kruse Blunck Architecture

General Contractor:
Taylor Ball

Structural:
Charles Saul Engineering

Mechanical / Electrical:
Alvine & Associates

Collaboration:
NA

Photographer:
Farshid Assassi

This project was designed to serve two purposes: first, to add a new facility capable of providing adequate accommodation for the athletics staff the existing sports complex; second, to construct a new ticket office and multi-media auditorium. At the same time the project modernized an old building that formerly held athletic department offices, football locker rooms, and the athletic training facility.

The project required a radical rearranging and alteration of the interiors in order to integrate the new with the old and make the entire complex more functional.

The northern portion of the existing building was gutted back to the steel frame and shell to create a large open volume for weight training. The existing north wall was removed and replaced by a curved glass block wall crowned with a skylight, making the formerly dark north face into a new street facade for the athletic complex.

A grand common lobby connects the new building to the field side of the existing single story building.

The new structure acts as a keystone placed at both the geometric and functional center of the entire sports complex, cutting into the slopes of two artificial mounds used as terraces for spectators. The construction is built primarily from metal and glass, carefully rationed in such a way as to create the roof's geometric forms, which look as if they were resting gently upon a thick stone base.

Opening page, a barn-like auditorium hovers over the lobby, providing a subtle reference to the Iowa setting. The skylight spine shares daylight with the lobby and office balconies below. This page, from top, vicinity and site plans; the new addition provides a comfortable venue for recruiting, as well as events for alumni, donors, and supporters of the athletic programs.

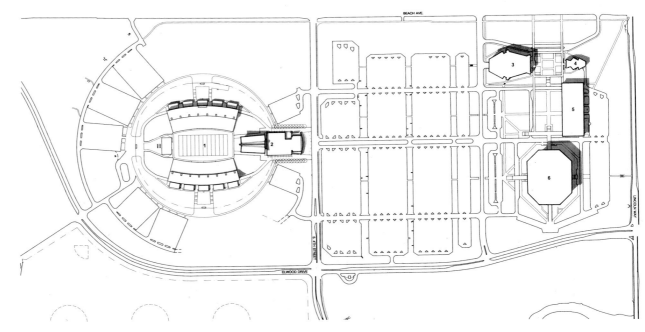

1 CYCLONE STADIUM - JACK TRICE FIELD
2 JACOBSON ATHLETIC OFFICE AND TRAINING FACILITY
3 C.Y. STEPHENS AUDITORIUM
4 J.W. FISHER THEATER
5 SHEMAN CONTINUING EDUCATION BUILDING
6 JAMES H. HILTON COLISEUM

NORTH

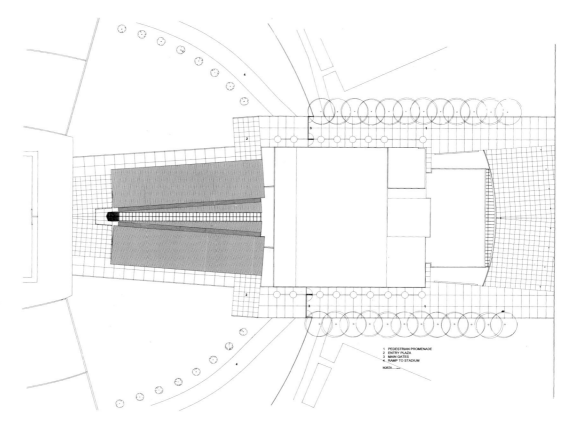

1 PEDESTRIAN PROMENADE
2 ENTRY PLAZA
3 MAIN GATES
4 RAMP TO STADIUM

NORTH

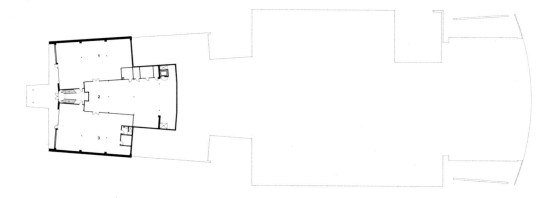

From top, ground floor
plan, first floor plan and
second floor plan;
the glazed south facade
overlooks the end zone
of the adjacent football
stadium.

1 STORAGE
2 MECHANICAL
3 MAINTENANCE

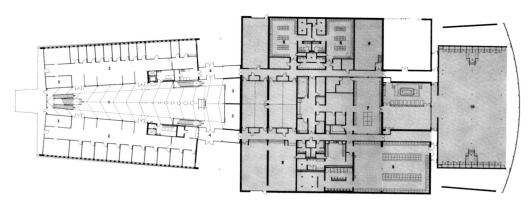

1 LIGHT COURT
2 OFFICES
3 CONFERENCE
4 ENTRY
5 EXISTING LOCKER ROOM
6 NEW LOCKER ROOM
7 ATHLETIC TRAINING FACILITY
8 EQUIPMENT STORAGE
9 MECHANICAL
10 WEIGHT TRAINING

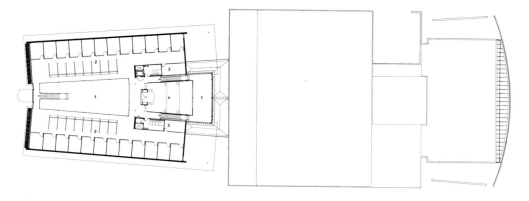

N

1 LIGHT COURT BELOW
2 OFFICES
3 CONFERENCE
4 AUDITORIUM

Right, sunscreens and overhangs protect the major south glazing. Below left, the building's lounges, conference rooms, and deck overlook the stadium, and serve as skyboxes for spectators on game days. Below right, daylight activates the weight room through the skylight wedge atop the glass block arc forming the new north end of the facility. Opposite page, the back-lit north wall illuminates the facility through its translucent glass- block construction, creating a dynamic new identity at the street.

Iowa City, Iowa,
1998

Melrose Avenue
Parking Ramp
University of Iowa

Date Completed:
1998

Owner:
State Board of Regents, State of
Iowa, University of Iowa

Ground Area:
2.56 acres

Constructed Area:
346,260 Gross Square Feet (675
cars)
(parking, medical records storage,
shell office space, critical care unit)

Architectural Design:
Herbert Lewis Kruse Blunck
Architecture

General Contractor:
McComas Lacina Construction Co.

Parking / Structural:
Desman Associates

Mechanical / Electrical:
Hansen Lind Meyer Engineering

Cost Estimator:
CPMI, Inc.

Collaboration:
NA

Photographers:
Barbara Karant, Cameron Campbell

This project is a car park situated near a university hospital, a sports facility annexed to the campus, and a housing estate. This new car park does not just provide temporary shelter for cars, it also fits into the urban context like a technological container by means of elements designed to carefully conceal its own function. A perforated stainless steel system incorporated in almost all the facades is used to camouflage the cars, while at the same time clearly indicating the public entrances. This design feature also makes it possible to create a simultaneously dynamic and neutral element to smoothly knit the new building into the urban context, which features a moderate lack of functional homogeneity.

In actual fact, the complex does not just (or so much) hold a total of 675 cars, it also contains a medical archives, areas for expanding the local hospital offices, a garage for medical emergency units, and pedestrian, underground, and overhead passage ways.

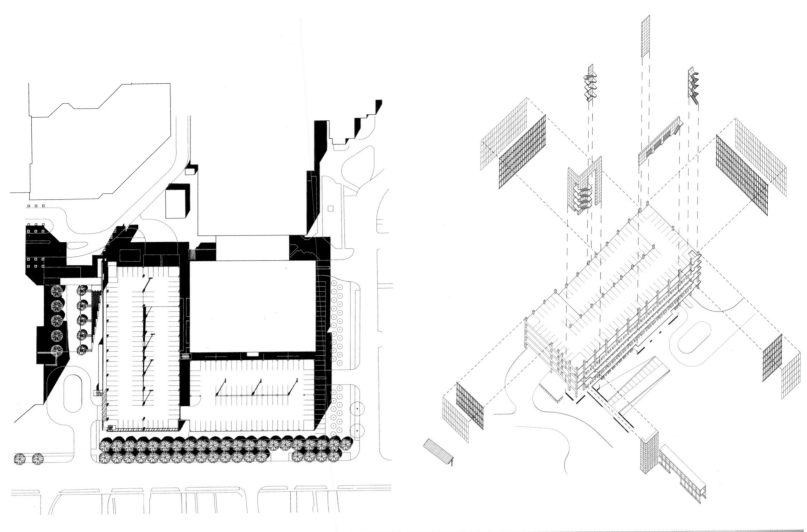

Opening page, the main elevator/stair core juxtaposes a massive cast-in-place concrete structural wall against the lacy steel window system.
Opposite page clockwise, site plan; axonometric view showing elements appended to the structure; the south facade is veiled in a mirror-finish, custom-perforated stainless steel screen. The screen wraps the most public faces of the ramp, and is removed in the landscaped courtyard to reveal the working of the structure.
Left, view from the southeast.

The cast-in-place stair and elevated pedestrian connection.

West Des Moines, Iowa, 1997

M.C. Ginsberg - Objects of Art

Date Completed:
1997

Owner:
Mark Ginsberg

Ground Area:
NA - existing space remodel

Constructed Area:
3,000 Gross Square Feet

Architectural Design:
Herbert Lewis Kruse Blunck
Architecture

General Contractor:
Holcomb Corporation

Mechanical / Electrical:
Stroth Corporation

Millwork:
Lisac Millwork

Custom Glass:
Two Rivers Glass and Door, Inc.

Ornamental Iron:
Hawk Metal Products, Inc.

Collaboration:
NA

Photographer:
Farshid Assassi

This project for a jewellery and fine accessories boutique stemmed from the need to create the right kind of surrounding environment for precious objects made of a variety of materials, such as gold, silver, precious stones, and porcelain, and to bring out their intrinsic features with delicate precision. It was decided to use materials like raw plaster, unfinished concrete, sandblasted steel, unfinished maple plywood, and extruded plastic, all strikingly different from the appearance of the goods on sale. The colours are deliberately neutral, the light is controlled with great elegance, and the displays are all tastefully designed.

The gallery, formerly a shoe shop in a strip mall in the city suburbs, is constructed out of building systems which can be easily dismantled and then reassembled if the shop plans to relocate when the rental contract expires.

Opening page, sculpture, art, and jewelry are set off by the austerity and neutrality of the spaces and the palette of materials.
This page, clockwise, looking from the rear toward the front of the shop, the entrance is concealed by the central drum, creating complexity in the circulation patterns; adjustable-height display cubes and shelves are wall-mounted between panels of cement board.
Opposite page top, a central drum of translucent extruded plastic creates a stage for display.
Opposite page bottom, maple panels create intimate stages for a gallery-like display of jewelry and art.

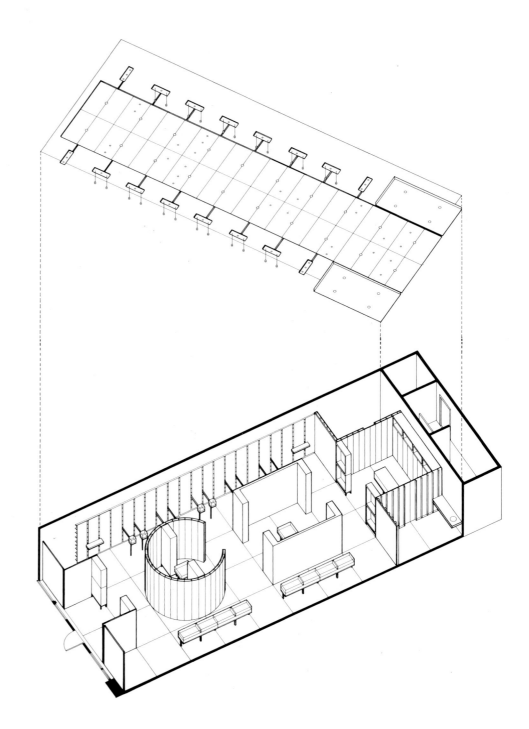

Axonometric view. Below, private meeting room is created by metal stud walls sheathed in extruded plastic -simple materials finished in a unique way create a foil for the objects of art. Opposite page, glass cubes supported on steel tubes create quiet boxes for display of jewelry and art.

Meredith Corporate Headquarters Expansion

Date Completed:
1998

Owner:
Meredith Corporation

Ground Area:
2.21 acres

Constructed Area:
185,000 Gross Square Feet (office)
90,000 Gross Square Feet (parking)

Architectural Design:
Herbert Lewis Kruse Blunck
Architecture

General Contractor:
Neumann Brothers

Structural:
Shuck-Britson, Inc.

Mechanical / Electrical:
Alvine & Associates

Energy:
Weidt Group

Plant Selection:
Heard Gardens

Collaboration:
NA

Photographer:
Farshid Assassi

The new building, a 185,000-square-foot extension over four levels of the Meredith Corporation, is a landmark for the west entrance to downtown Des Moines. The L-shaped complex extends beyond the size of a single block to create a self-contained urban space, Meredith Square. In this case, there seems to be a crucial need to construct a topos out of the road network, capable of providing a sense of civic identity and of constructing landmarks for the local community. Urban systems featuring rather rigid stylistic designs use building blocks to create new meeting places, sheltered, functional, collective agoras capable of keeping up with the rhythm and pace of American cities.

A landscaped area adaptable to future extensions the size of an entire block has been created to the west of the complex. On the east, a second garden of the same size will form the first part of Gateway Park, currently at the drawing board stage, envisioned to be one of the key landmarks on the cityscape.

The new building is connected to the old construction by a skywalk system, while there is a car park with room for 300 vehicles below ground.

The facades are fitted with sunscreens and light shelves to protect wide open glass spaces, while letting in sunlight used for naturally lighting the interiors. This system has made it possible to reduce standard electricity consumption.

The patterns of the fenestration are reiterated in the enclosed interiors: wide full-height spaces crossed by overhead walks that stand out due to the extensive use of metallic shades of grey contrasting with the bright red monumental staircase in the background.

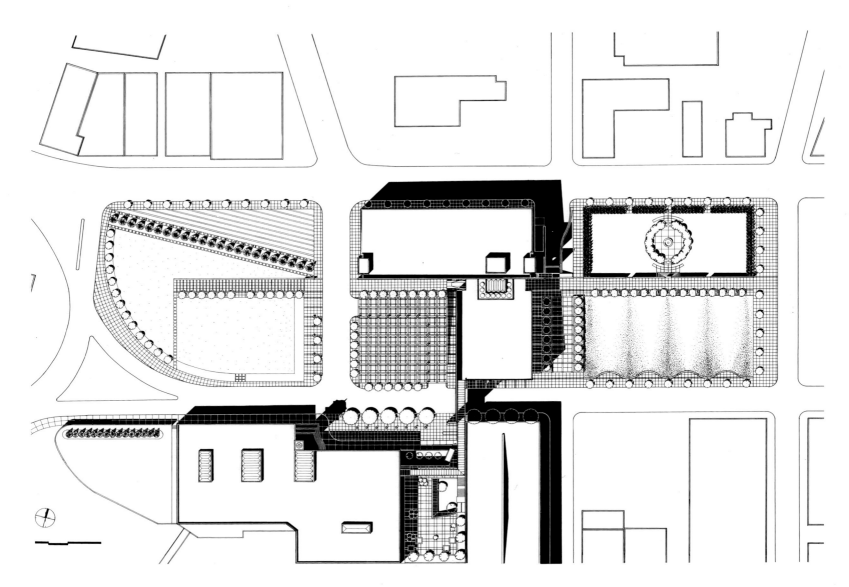

Opening page, east entry to the central atrium. The precast concrete and aluminum facade of the south wing is juxtaposed with the aluminum panel and flush glazed stair tower to the north.
Above, site plan of the corporate campus, including the existing corporate headquarters to the south and the L-shaped expansion to the north. The inter-relationships between the new and existing buildings help create an entry plaza for the downtown area beyond.
Below, floor plans.

1. Open office
2. Office (Typ.)
3. Conference room
4. Restroom
5. Atrium
6. Break room
7. Board room
8. Video Conference room

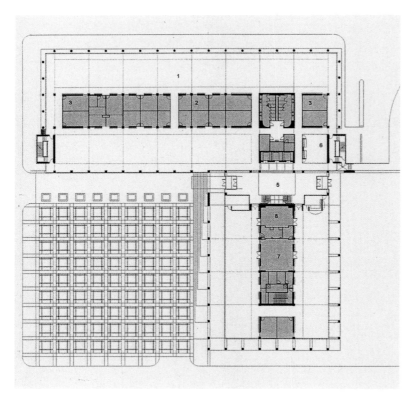

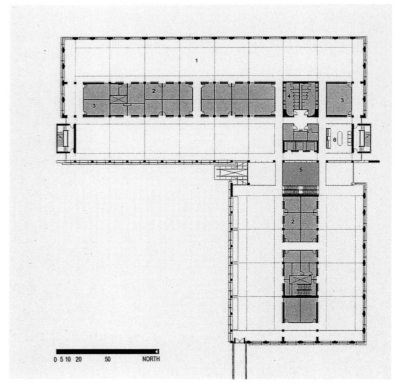

0 5 10 20   50   NORTH

Above, the corporate
campus with the west
landscape block in the
foreground. The
century-old water tower
of the existing building
provides a focus for the
urban space.

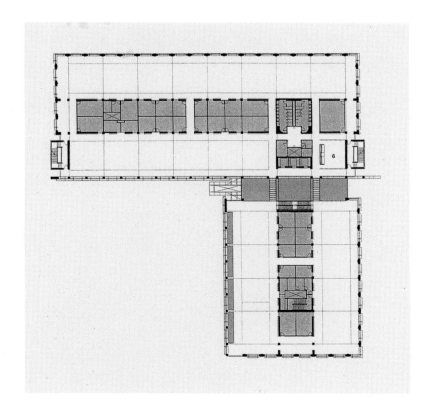

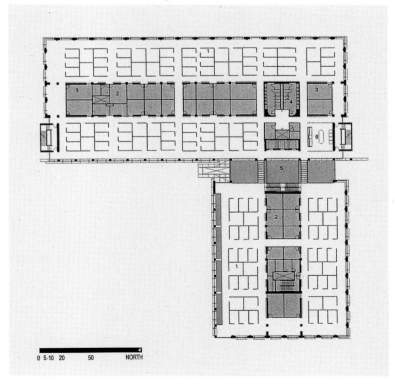

Above left, view of the east entry in the evening. The interior atrium and bridges are visible within.
Above right, west entry plaza.
Right, the arm of the west elevation reaches over the street to connect to the existing structures and create a gateway into the central business district.
Below, the building stays partially lit in the evening and serves as a welcoming gate for those entering the downtown area.
Opposite page clockwise, lightly scaled bridges with translucent glass floors cross the central atrium; the central stair in the atrium features a suspended glass wall; the lower level of the central stair appears to be suspended from steel verticals; detail of the intersection between the suspended glass wall and bridges in the central atrium.

Opposite page, central atrium with bridges at the third and fourth levels. The city skyline is visible beyond the employee lounge space. Left, a pedestrian "skywalk" over the street below connects the existing corporate headquarters with the new expansion.

Below, daylight "slot" in the third and fourth level floors adjacent to the exterior wall. Bottom, an open conferencing area on the fourth level takes advantage of a panoramic view of the existing corporate headquarters and the distant river valley.

Marakon Associates

Date Completed:
1999

Owner:
Marakon Associates

Ground Area:
NA - existing space remodel

Constructed Area:
8,500 Gross Square Feet

Architectural Design:
Herbert Lewis Kruse Blunck
Architecture

General Contractor:
Dinwiddle Construction Company

Structural:
Structural Engineers Collaboration

Mechanical:
Tommy Siu Associates

Electrical:
David Szeto & Associates

Collaboration:
Robert Gyori Architect

Photographer:
Farshid Assassi

This project is for the renovation of Marakon Associates offices in San Francisco, located on the top two floors of a services building in the heart of this Californian city.

The spaces have been redesigned to fit in with Marakon's new approach to the work market, emphasizing on greater emotional involvement on the part of its staff.

Great attention is focused on the basic idea that the proper construction and harmonious design of interiors can play a key role in the successful careers of its staff, who are encouraged to engage in team work. The design emphasizes interaction between real spaces and functions by using flexible systems capable of adapting physical-visual connections to its users' requirements, gearing them to the need to maintain good communication links.

A sequence of perspectives through the space starts at the deliberately dark elevator lobby, continues through a compressed entry hall, and terminates in the explosive volumes of the reception court through delicate transparent shielding opening up to a panoramic view of the perimeter terrace.

The attempt to create a real sense of belonging in company staff is underlined by the creation of a central reception court, an area everyone is both visually and physically involved in, surrounded by carefully designed and arranged internal partitions. This space, which usually acts as a visitors' waiting area, turns into the focus of the company's social activities once-a-week, as in the case of the perimeter terrace used for exterior conferencing and dining purposes, and open to all the staff.

The internal partitions are designed around an "open door" policy; transparent and translucent walls provide both optical and emotional connection between the different areas, concealed sliding doors alter the way things are visually perceived and play down the separation between different levels of staff, instilling the Marakon offices with a diffused sense of openness and accessibility.

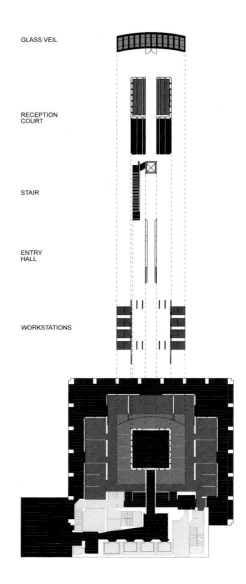

GLASS VEIL

RECEPTION
COURT

STAIR

ENTRY
HALL

WORKSTATIONS

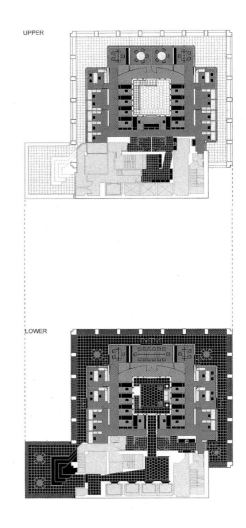

UPPER

LOWER

Opening page, a curved wall of patterned glass maintains a sense of openness, while providing the necessary privacy to the boardroom. Custom bud vases are graced with fresh flowers each week when the office entertains clients. Above, the boardroom and exterior terrace take advantage of the San Francisco skyline in the distance. Right, floor plans.

A glass opening
between the
boardroom and the
office beyond visually
opens the two spaces.

The main aisleway
visually extends
through the private
office at the end.

Smaller workstations
are enhanced by the
view of the city and
bay in the distance.

Conferencing areas are
extended outside on
the perimeter terrace.

Opposite page, the
finely detailed
reception court creates
a showroom for the
Sol Lewitt prints that
inspired the
architecture.

Center Street Park and Ride Facility

Date Completed:
1998

Owner:
City of Des Moines

Ground Area:
2.8 acres

Constructed Area:
600,000 Gross Square Feet (1,815 cars)

Architectural Design:
Herbert Lewis Kruse Blunck Architecture

General Contractor:
Taylor Ball

Parking / Structural:
Desman Associates

Civil:
Bishop Engineering

Mechanical / Electrical:
Krishna Engineering Consultants, Inc.

Cost Estimator:
CPMI

Collaboration:
NA

Photographer:
Farshid Assassi

The Center Street Park & Ride Facility in Des Moines tackles themes connected with the smooth running of urban machinery, clearly indicating, and solving, some of its most tricky problems. The idea hinges around finding a concrete means of helping reduce inner-city road traffic in the central business district, and providing temporary rest facilities for workers at the physical limits of this area.

The building provides the chance to construct a multi-purpose complex capable of smoothly guiding the natural and induced growth of public facilities. Primary functions include a large car park, a day-care facility for one hundred children, and the metro bus station providing links with the downtown neighbourhood.

This is a simple, austere and, at the same time, warm and welcoming design; the building fits neatly into the urban context, in the name of both industrial-type architecture and its own specific function and intrinsic meaning.

The facility meets carefully gauged site conditions and a detailed urban master plan, facing up to the surrounding city to serve various purposes: an urban square, a monumental, almost instructive entrance landmark to the downtown area, and a technological machine serving the community.

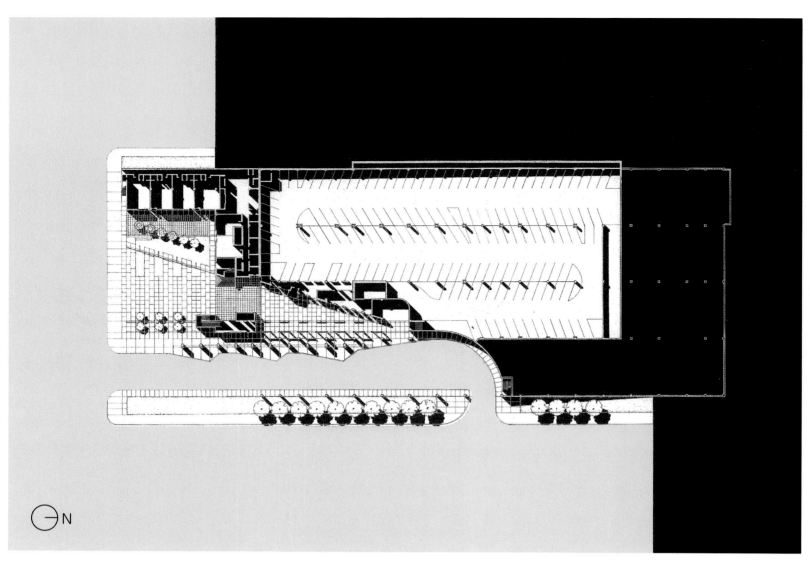

Opening page, the metro station canopy emerges from the south facade alongside the transparent stair and elevator tower. The perforated screen behind announces the facility to commuters exiting the central business district. Above, street-level plan with the daycare to the upper left and the metro station to the lower left.

Right, seven-foot tall letters announce the facility entrance. The letters rest on cantilevered concrete beams which penetrate the perforated stainless steel screen. Opposite page, the southern stair tower, viewed through the perforated stainless steel screen, shows references to the early modernism of Gropius and the Bauhaus.

This page clockwise, the main elevations of the garage are composed of galvanized grates and stretched chain link; the metro station; the approach to the facility focuses on the mammoth "PARK" sign, reflected in its stainless billboard. The downtown skyline is the backdrop to the view when approaching the facility.
Opposite page, the two stair towers viewed across the plaza above the daycare.

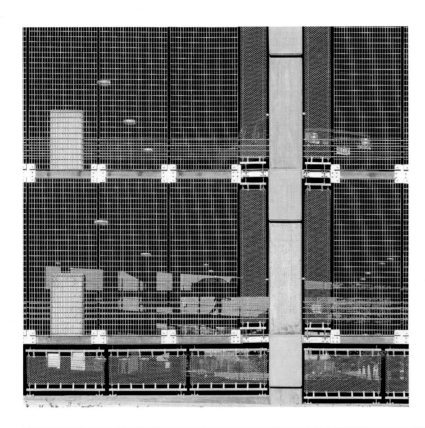

Sticks, Inc. Studio and Factory

Date Completed:
2000

Owner:
Sticks, Inc.

Ground Area:
6.5 acres

Constructed Area:
27,000 Square Feet

Architectural Design:
Herbert Lewis Kruse Blunck
Architecture

General Contractor:
Neumann Brothers, Inc.

Structural:
Charles Saul Engineering

Mechanical:
Wolin & Associates

Electrical:
Wolin Electric

Interior Steel:
Parker Welding

**Pre-Engineered Building
System:**
Butler Manufacturing Company

Stud Framing:
Kennedy & Company

Precast:
Swanson Gentleman, Inc.

Glass & Glazing:
Forman Ford Glass Company

Curtain Walls:
Wasau Metals

Doors:
Lisac Millwork

Door Finish:
Sticks, Inc.

Collaboration:
Sticks

Photographer:
Farshid Assassi

Sticks, Inc. is a rapidly expanding artists studio specialising in the design and manufacture of contemporary art objects made of fallen timber. The studio's headquarters and production pavilion stand in the bounds of a mature oak grove on the western outskirts of the city of Des Moines.

The symbolic centre and focus of the architectural design is a set of closed spaces designed for work purposes and geared to providing the necessary and indispensable stimulus for greater manufacturing efficiency, growth, and operating flexibility. Great attention has in fact been paid to the location of the pavilion and position of its architectural structures. Built at the highest part of the property, this facility stands out due to the clever pattern of openings towards the outside and their position in relation to the sun exposure.

The pre-engineered steel structure is flaunted outside the compact external curtain features, made of metal panels and tilt-up precast concrete, to set the rhythm of the loggia incorporated in the west facade.

Opening page, natural daylight from the north curtain wall provides ideal lighting for the painters working in this area. Built-up metal stud columns, beams, and struts transfer lateral loads back to the Butler structure.
Above, carefully sited in a grove of mature oak trees, the north glass wall allows views out to the wooded site and natural daylight to permeate deep into the open plan.
Right, large openings in the mezzanine offices reinforce the Owner's democratic attitudes towards collaboration with the artists they employ. The layout of blackboard panels corresponds to the exterior doors embellished with Sticks, surface design.

Metal stud walls clad with perforated raw steel panels and lined with clear plastic panels enclose the spray booth and allow for natural daylight. The large perforated metal supply duct is in the foreground.

Raw steel plate partitions define work areas and production circulation. The walls provide an outlet for the artists' impromptu sketches.

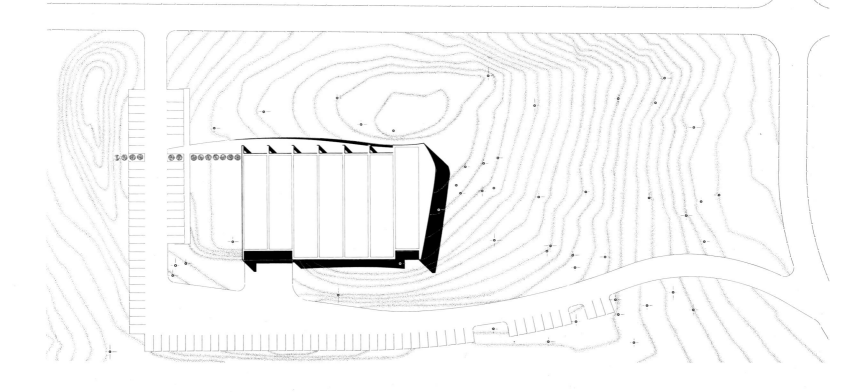

Above, site plan. Right, at the end of the rhythm of steel plate partitions, large glass openings visually connect the wood shop to the remainder of the production flow. The monochromatic palette provides a neutral canvas for Sticks' lively art. Opposite page, the rigid steel frame structure extends beyond the building to form an exterior loggia. Large wood doors and transoms marked with Sticks' artistry articulate the facade.

List of Works
Significant Projects
1961 to present

St. Paul Presbyterian Church, Johnston, Iowa

Brady Motorfrate Building, Des Moines, Iowa

Brenton Student Center, Simpson College, Indianola, Iowa

Black Oaks Office Building, Des Moines, Iowa

Welch Junior High School, Ames, Iowa

Student Center, Drake University, Des Moines, Iowa

Northwood Elementary School, Ames, Iowa

Vacation House, Lake Panorama, Iowa

Home Federal Savings and Loan, Ingersoll Branch, Des Moines, Iowa

Des Moines Register & Tribune, Executive Office Remodel, Des Moines, Iowa

Continental-Western Insurance Building, Urbandale, Iowa

College of Nursing, University of Iowa, Iowa City, Iowa

Blank Center for the Performing Arts, Simpson College, Indianola, Iowa

Dial Center for Computer Science, Drake University, Des Moines, Iowa

Capital City State Bank, Hickman Road Branch, Des Moines, Iowa

Ames High School Fine Arts Wing, Ames, Iowa

Home Federal Savings and Loan, West Des Moines Branch, West Des Moines, Iowa

Dallas County State Bank, Redfield, Iowa

Dallas County State Bank, Adel, Iowa

American Republic Insurance Warehouse Building, Des Moines, Iowa

Prestige Jewelers and Distributors, Des Moines, Iowa

Equity Dynamics Office Suite, Des Moines, Iowa

Martin Luther King, Jr. Elementary School, Des Moines, Iowa

Learning Resource Center, Central College, Pella, Iowa

Home State Bank Drive-Up Facility, Jefferson Iowa

Dwinell Residence, Des Moines, Iowa

Brenton Bank & Trust Company, Urbandale Branch, Urbandale, Iowa

American Federal Savings & Loan, South Side Branch, Des Moines, Iowa

Northwestern Bell Office & Equipment Building, Marshalltown, Iowa

Home State Bank, Jefferson, Iowa

American Federal Savings & Loan, Merle Hay Branch, Des Moines, Iowa

South Des Moines National Bank, Wakonda Branch, Des Moines, Iowa

Macomb Savings & Loan, Macomb, Illinois

Holiday Inn/Bandag Headquarters, Muscatine, Iowa

Des Moines Public Library, South Side Branch, Des Moines, Iowa

Brenton Bank & Trust, Cedar Rapids, Iowa

Eyler Residence, West Des Moines, Iowa

Des Moines Register & Tribune, Newsroom Remodeling, Des Moines, Iowa

College of Design, Iowa State University, Ames, Iowa

Brenton Bank & Trust, Cedar Rapids, Iowa

Valley National Bank Building Restoration, Des Moines, Iowa

Northwestern Bell Data Center, Des Moines, Iowa

Gartner Residence, Des Moines, Iowa

Civic Center and Nollen Plaza, Des Moines, Iowa

Ballantine Residence, Des Moines, Iowa

Dial Corporation, Des Moines, Iowa

Des Moines Orthopedic Surgeons, Des Moines, Iowa

Cory Residence, Okoboji, Iowa

Clause Residence, Largo Vista, Texas

Shiffler Residence, Des Moines, Iowa

Pioneer Hi-Bred International, Central Division Headquarters, Johnston, Iowa

Meredith Corporation Additions and Remodeling, Des Moines, Iowa

Tifereth Israel Synagogue Interior Renovation, Des Moines, Iowa

Brenton State Bank, Granger, Iowa

American Federal Savings & Loan, Ingersoll Branch, Des Moines, Iowa

American Federal Savings & Loan, Locust Mall Branch, Des Moines, Iowa

Library Addition, Iowa State University, Ames, Iowa

Des Moines Register & Tribune, Skywalk Lobby, Des Moines, Iowa

AID Insurance Services, Eden Prairie, Minnesota

Valone Residence, Des Moines, Iowa

Pederson-Autry Residence, Des Moines, Iowa

Des Moines Register & Tribune, 8th Floor Remodel, Des Moines, Iowa

Wakonda Club Addition and Remodeling, Des Moines, Iowa

Hub Tower/Kaleidoscope at the Hub, Des Moines, Iowa

Capitol Center Office Development, Des Moines, Iowa

Regency Park Office Building, Omaha, Nebraska

Meredith Corporation Conference Center, Des Moines, Iowa

Black Engineering Building, Iowa State University, Ames, Iowa

Genesis, Ltd. Office Remodeling, Des Moines, Iowa

Faith Lutheran Church, Clive, Iowa

Adams, Howe & Zoss Law Office, Des Moines, Iowa

Meastique Jewels, Kansas City, Missouri

GenEx Office Remodeling Phase II, Des Moines, Iowa

Allied Group Lobbies and Skywalk Extension, Des Moines, Iowa

Norwest Financial, Inc. Headquarters Vertical Expansion, Des Moines, Iowa

North Campus Parking and Chilled Water Facility, University of Iowa, Iowa City, Iowa

Des Moines Art Center Playspace, Des Moines, Iowa

Veteran's Auditorium Concourse and Skywalk, Des Moines, Iowa

Faegre & Benson Law Office, Des Moines, Iowa

Pulmonary Medicine, P.C., West Des Moines, Iowa

Martin Luther King, Jr. Elementary School Science Addition, Des Moines, Iowa

Kruse/Berg Kruse Residence, West Des Moines, Iowa

Iowa Teleproduction Center, West Des Moines, Iowa

Bradshaw Fowler Proctor & Fairgrave Law Office, Des Moines, Iowa

Whitfield & Eddy Law Office, Des Moines, Iowa

Perishable Distributors of Iowa Addition, Ankeny, Iowa

B.A.D. Productions, Des Moines, Iowa

MidAmerica Savings Bank, Des Moines, Iowa

Medical Laboratory Firestairs, University of Iowa, Iowa City, Iowa

Kautz Plaza, University of Iowa, Iowa City, Iowa

Finkbine Mansion Remodel/Renovation, Des Moines, Iowa

Recreation Building Addition, University of Iowa, Iowa City, Iowa

Meyocks & Priebe Office Interiors, West Des Moines, Iowa

Bankers Trust Company, Downtown Branch Remodel, Des Moines, Iowa

Engineering Animation Headquarters, Ames, Iowa

Homeland Savings Bank, Urbandale Branch, Urbandale, Iowa

Athletic Office and Training Facility, Iowa State University, Ames, Iowa

Praxair Distribution, Ankeny, Iowa

American College Testing Program Site Development, Iowa City, Iowa

Coffee House, Cornell College, Mount Vernon, Iowa

Helmick Penthouse, Des Moines, Iowa

Wallace Hall Renovation and Addition, Simpson College, Indianola, Iowa

Weight Training Facility, Iowa State University, Ames, Iowa

Simon Estes Riverfront Amphitheater, Des Moines, Iowa

Club Chris Greenhouse, Orchard Place, Des Moines, Iowa

M.C. Ginsberg Objects of Art, West Des Moines, Iowa

Schaeffer Hall Restoration, University of Iowa, Iowa City, Iowa

Mauck + Associates, Des Moines, Iowa

Meredith Corporate Expansion, Des Moines, Iowa

Melrose Avenue Parking Facility, University of Iowa, Iowa City, Iowa

Equitable Insurance Headquarters, Des Moines, Iowa

Teachout Building Restoration, Des Moines, Iowa

Still Residence Renovation, Des Moines, Iowa

Des Moines Art Center Maytag Reflecting Pool Restoration, Des Moines, Iowa

Des Moines City Council Chambers Restoration, Des Moines, Iowa

Zimmerman, Laurent & Richardson, Des Moines, Iowa

Center Street Park and Ride Facility, Des Moines, Iowa

Sticks, Inc., Des Moines, Iowa

Marakon Associates, San Francisco, California

Friendship Court, Palmer College of Chiropractic, Davenport, Iowa

Profile of Firm

STAFF

Charles E. Herbert, FAIA
Calvin F. Lewis, FAIA
Rod G. Kruse, FAIA
Kirk V. Blunck, FAIA

Paul D. Mankins, AIA
Todd Garner, AIA
Timothy Hickman
Greg Lehman, AIA
Richard Seely, AIA

Jim Dwinell, AIA
John Locke, AIA
Doug Frey, AIA
J. Mark Schmidt, AIA, CSI
Emily Gloe-Donovan, AIA
Thomas Hilton, AIA
Brian Lindgren, AIA
Brett Mendenhall, AIA
Erin Olson-Douglas, AIA
Channing Swanson, AIA
Jill Swanson, AIA
Rob Whitehead, AIA
Brett Douglas, ASLA
James Hoff, AIA
Ellen Kyhl, AIA
Carl Rogers
Josh Baker
Michael Bechtel
Cheung Chan
Brad Hartman
Khalid Khan
Brad Kramer
Joshua Lekwa
Matt Niebuhr
Matt Rodekamp
Jonathan Sloan
Ann Sobiech-Munson
Tom Trapp
Kerry Weig

Kay Boller
David Nandell
Julie Severson
Julie Liening
Sommer Reece

Herbert Lewis Kruse Blunck Architecture is a continuation of the Charles Herbert and associates architectural firm established in Des Moines, Iowa in 1961. This collaboration of talents continues a tradition of excellence in master planning, architectural design, interior design, and landscape architecture – a tradition that has generated some of the Midwest region's most significant and enduring buildings.

The Firm displays a commitment to serve its clients by listening carefully and working diligently to address their needs. The Firm's 50-person size, coupled with four decades of experience, allows it to generate a wide variety of projects, ranging from $100 million multi-use complexes to the smallest interior projects. A seasoned architectural staff, working with talented interns and students, ensures that the architecture created is a blend of both time-tested and innovative techniques and materials. The Firm can assemble and lead a large and diverse consultant team while working closely with an owner to facilitate accurate and immediate communication. As a result, Herbert Lewis Kruse Blunck Architecture is large enough to provide each client and project with special care and attention.

Although the majority of the completed work has been in Iowa, past projects are located in 13 states, from California to New York. The work has been published in most of the professional architectural and consumer media, providing many of these clients and projects with valuable exposure. Moreover, Herbert Lewis Kruse Blunck Architecture has been recognized by peer and user groups for its commitment to design excellence and innovation. This recognition includes five National Honor Awards presented by the American Institute of Architects; four of those were received in the last four years. The Firm was selected from the nation's 25,000 architectural practices to receive the American Institute of Architects' 2001 Architecture Firm Award – the Institute's highest honor for a design practice.

The diversity of the work accomplished over the past 40 years is a testament to the Firm's philosophy that deals with each client and project as a special opportunity to listen and learn by closely working together. The result is a portfolio of sensible and successful design solutions that are of lasting value to both clients and communities.